FUN Net
FUNDraising
Be a Good Ancestor

CLIFFORD TODD

FunNet Fundraising — Be A Good Ancestor
Copyright © 2022 Clifford Todd. All Rights Reserved.

Moment Time®, FUN Net™, and BE DO HAVE GIVE™
are trademarks owned by Clifford Todd.

No part of this book may be reproduced or transmitted in any form by any means, electronic or mechanical, including photocopying, recording or by any information storage and retrieval system, without specific written permission from the publisher or copyright holder. The scanning, uploading, and distribution of this book via the Internet or via any other means without the permission of the publisher or copyright holder are illegal and punishable by law. Please purchase only authorized electronic editions, and do not participate in or encourage electronic piracy of copyrighted materials.

This book is not intended to diagnose, treat, or cure any illness. The author and publisher accept no responsibility for such use. Conditions requiring proper medical attention should be referred to a physician. If you require medical attention, please consult with your medical practitioner.

Financial projections are an example only. Your income and your teams' incomes are solely the results of your personal efforts and are neither implied nor guaranteed by the author or publisher.

Book Cover and Interior Design by Francine Eden Platt
Eden Graphics, Inc. • www.edengraphics.net

BookWise Publishing
Bookwisepublishing.com

ISBN #978-1-60645-312-4

Version **07/14/2022**

DEDICATION

To Sloane,

Born February 21, 2022, at 7:23 a.m. EST

Dear Sloane,

You are a precious child of the Divine Spirit born into a mortal world that is at serious risk of mass extinction of its sentient living beings.

I am dedicating this book to you with the trust that you see your grandchildren have babies just as lovely as you are.

My pledge to you is to dedicate my best efforts and highest professionalism to preserving the life sustainability of Mother Earth so that you may experience this joy.

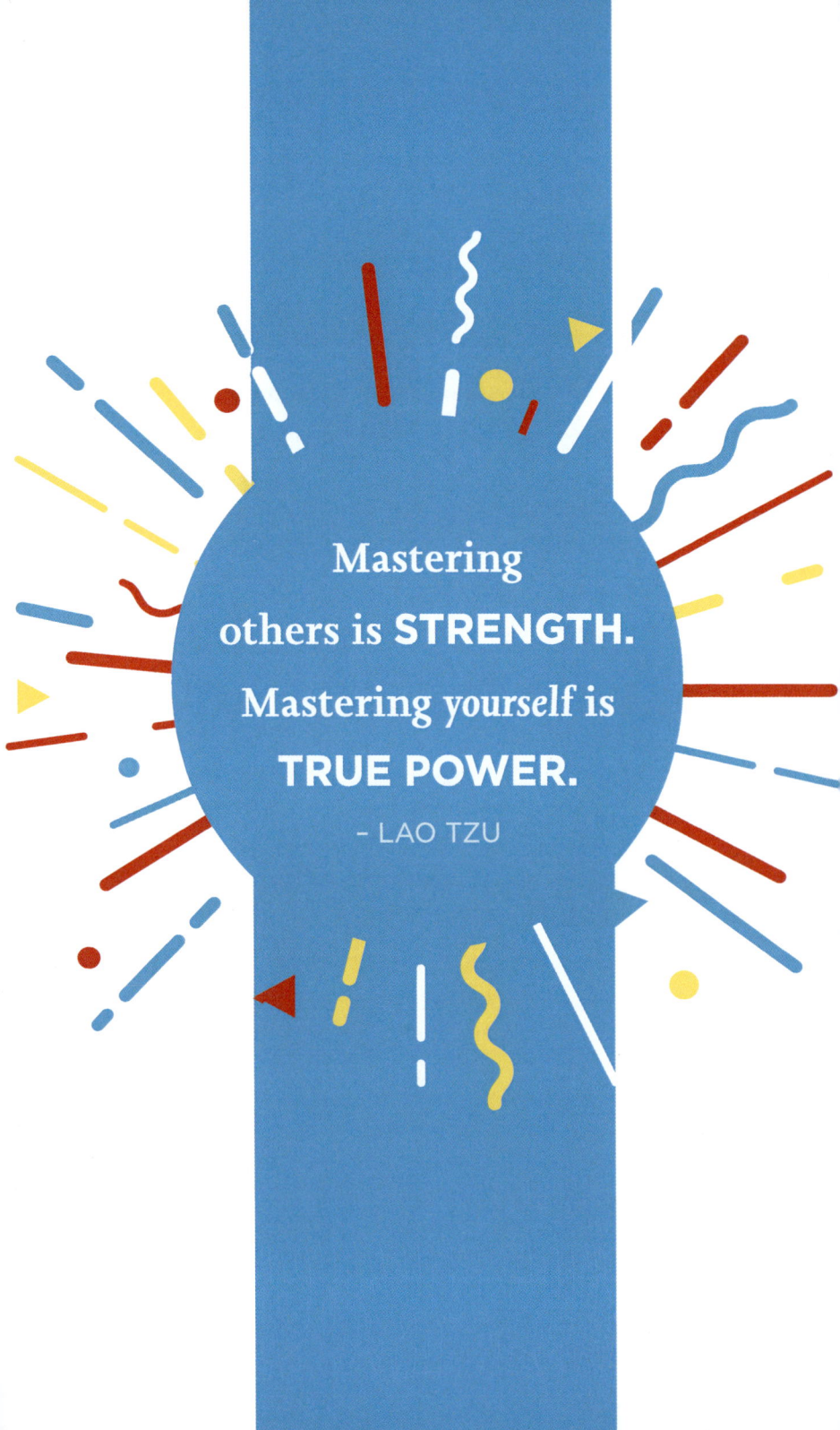

TABLE OF CONTENTS

PREFACE: Be Passionately Curious.....................vii

   I.   Energy 1

   II.   Love: The Most Powerful Energy 3

   III.   Set Your Intentions 5
        Your Intention for Your Life
        Your Intention for All Life for Centuries to Come

   IV.   Spiritual Beliefs: How I Believe Universe Works .. 7
        The Law of Unity
        The Law of Cause and Effect
        The Law of Circulation

   V.   Material World Actions: Be Do Have Give 11

   VI.   An Unforgettable, Infallible and Unstoppable Ongoing Fundraiser: Green Fuel Global 25

   VII.   What Clifford's Guides Taught Him 31

   VIII.   Teaching Affiliates FUN Net Fundraising 33
        What are the Attributes of an Ideal Affiliate?
        Let the Tools Do the Work

   IX.   My Journey 37

RESOURCES... 39

> I have no particular talents.
> I am only **PASSIONATELY CURIOUS.**
>
> – ALFRED EINSTEIN

AUTHOR'S NOTES

The Einstein quote challenges you to extract the maximum impact reading and studying this book can have in and on your life. So have fun, stay consciously aware, and listen as the Divine Spirit gently nudges you.

BE curious and listen for ways you can best bridge being both a physical being and a spiritual being at the same time.

BE curious and listen for ways you can see things as energy in motion when they appear physically static and solid,

BE curious and listen for ways you can satisfy three separate intentions and serve three separate causes simultaneously with one set of actions.

BE PASSIONATELY CURIOUS AND AWARE as the Divine Spirit reveals what they may be planning for you and your life as you live fully into BEing your Authentic YOU.

PREFACE

The Gettysburg Address is arguably the best-known speech in American history. It begins with the words, "Four score and seven years ago . . ." referring to the signing of the Declaration of Independence. President Lincoln goes on to raise the question of whether "This nation, conceived in liberty and dedicated to the principle that all men are created equal" will long endure.

Today, we, the human race, are arguably engaged in our own civil war, only now it's not brother against brother; it's the greed of humans who are polluting the planet and destroying the planet's lungs—its rainforests—against the efforts of environmentalists and climatologists who are fighting to preserve life's sustainability on Mother Earth for centuries to come. This civil war can destroy life sustainability on our planet. But it's not too late.

The real heroes of this civil war are the many professionals that contribute to the general population's awareness that a true war effort is needed and the many customers of Green Fuel Global that are fighting against pollution from their own vehicles.

I wrote this book specifically to support their efforts in this war to save life viability on Mother Earth. Please join us to save your future generations too. Thank you.

> If you want to find the **SECRETS OF THE UNIVERSE**, think in terms of **ENERGY, FREQUENCY,** and **VIBRATIONS.**
>
> – NIKOLA TESLA

AUTHOR'S NOTES

Nikola Tesla (1856–1943), best known for his contributions to the design of alternating circuity (AC electricity), was a futurist. Nearing age 90, Tesla warned of the destruction that Man could create (e.g., nuclear war could happen).

Today collective human energy must be directed to assuring life sustainability on Mother Earth. Together we must stop destroying Earth's ability to sustain all life and assure life sustainability or experts (e.g., Bruce H. Lipton, Ph.D.) predict that all life on the planet will perish before the end of this century.

ENERGY

Energy is Everything. Everything is **Energy**. DNA extracted from fossils show that modern humans appeared intact on Earth about 200,000 years ago. Their skulls, DNA, and brains were just like ours are now.

Modern humans live with three primary energy centers: the earth's electrical and magnetic energies, their hearts, and their minds. They experience their thoughts, feelings, emotions, and beliefs consciously.

Quantum scientists agree that there is one universe and everything in it is energy. This is NOT a new concept. One hundred years ago Albert Einstein said, "Matter is an illusion, albeit a pervasive one." Beliefs based on energy and matter being separate are false. **It's all energy.** Every expression of energy produces an equal expression of energy. Energy always in motion creates the constantly evolving Universe.

Religious leaders also agree that there is only one infinite energy. There is no right or wrong. There is only our perception of infinite energy, filtered through our beliefs, which support believing in an Infinite Being most call **"God."** I call this source the **"Divine Spirit."**

In Tesla's words, to find the secrets of the Universe, think in terms of **"ENERGY, frequency, and vibrations."**

I believe the Divine Spirit created human beings in images reflecting itself. Look for the good in everything and everyone you see. Validate what's good in all you see.

Clifford Todd | 1

My book **BE DO HAVE GIVE**™ shows how to use your thoughts to create time and financial freedom. The purpose of this book is to help you integrate your financial life and your eternal spiritual life together as one integrated whole. You will soon discover that you reveal your spiritual qualities by how you use money.

How so is wrapped up in one question: **"What's the money for?"** I trust you can now, or soon will be, able to authentically say "I support myself, my family, my favorite causes, and preserving life for all sentient beings on Earth for centuries to come."

> And how will I confront each whom I meet? In only one way. In silence, and to myself, I will address him or her and say, **"I LOVE YOU."** Though spoken in silence, these words will **shine in my eyes,** unwrinkle my brow, bring a smile to my lips, and echo in my voice, and **his heart will be opened."** — OG MANDINO

AUTHOR'S NOTES

Og Mandino understood the concept of mirror neurons long before scientists identified them. In neuro-science terms, mirror neurons **in others' brains and hearts pick up and accurately interpret the energy our mirror neurons release.** Wikipedia defines it: "A mirror neuron is a neuron that fires both when an animal acts and when the animal observes the same action performed by another, thus the neuron mirrors the behavior of the other, as though the observer were acting."

You can connect with others and deepen the connections **before words are spoken.** When you send a sincere "I love you" out in silence, recipients who feel it will experience it and send it back to you.

It's energy causing an equal expression of energy.

LOVE:
THE MOST POWERFUL ENERGY

> When the **POWER OF LOVE** exceeds the love of power, the world will know **PEACE**.
> – JIMI HENDRIX

THE DIVINE SPIRIT IS LOVE. Love is the Divine Spirit. When people consciously grasp the fact that there is only one universe where Love exists and that everything in it is connected to everything else in it, then each person is in the Divine Spirit and the Divine Spirit is in each person. All people have the infinite power of unconditional LOVE to create whatever each person truly wants if everyone sustains that desire long enough for the Divine Spirit to rearrange itself in the desired image.

The collective cultural conditioning is that people are not good enough, powerful enough, or worthy enough to be the Divine Spirit directing how their lives flow out in the physical world where people see energy as real "things." These errors have been repeatedly passed on from one generation to the next throughout recorded history.

For thousands of years, civilizations have held their rich and powerful people in the highest esteem. It's as if the order of being was Do **Have** Be (somebody). When the order of living shifts to

Be Do Have, so **Being** is the **primary goal,** striving simultaneously for self-interests, one's loved causes, and preserving the planet's life self-sustainability for centuries to come is quite doable.

Being in the spiritual context of LOVE makes our lives most enjoyable.

> Somewhere, somehow, **SOMETHING INCREDIBLE** is waiting to be known. — CARL SAGAN

> The real voyage of discovery lies not in seeking new landscapes but in **HAVING NEW EYES.** — MARCEL PROUST

> Tell me sufficiently **WHY** I should do something, and I will **MOVE HEAVEN AND EARTH** to do it. — SOCRATES

SET YOUR INTENTIONS

ONE TO ACHIEVE what you want, and one for the planet.
People desire a better life. Your solution lies within your Earth-Heart-Mind resonance. Begin by asking yourself: a year from now, what would have had to have happened in my life, **personally and professionally,** and on Mother Earth for me to be happy with the results?

Specifically, what dangers must I eliminate? What strengths must I maximize? What opportunities must I capture? What relationships will I strengthen? Let go of? Again, what must I do in 2022 to be happy?

SET YOUR INTENTION(S). Lock in pictures of what you want in all arenas. For thoughts to become reality, they must form clear, concise, and **sustained patterns of energy.** Sustained long enough to condense into denser levels of experience. Desire, the energy of emotion, sustains your thought-seeds into reality you can see with your eyes.

As the magnetic energy of the Earth continues to descend, your creative energy effectively becomes more potent. The Earth's energy is also electrical. The electromagnetic energy of your heart (according to HeartMate research) is more powerful magnetically and electrically than your brain. In essence, your feelings and emotions are way more powerful than your thoughts in creating how your life flows and how effective you are in transforming it.

Clifford Todd | 5

Personal transformations begin global evolution. This book shows practical ways for people to improve their living conditions by **changing their thoughts, beliefs, and expectations.** Please explore how we can all express ourselves (how we can **BE DO HAVE GIVE**) together and enjoy *peace, freedom, power, love, happiness, and abundance,* while we simultaneously make the planet a safer place to **BE**.

YOU EXIST in many realms— many dimensions of existence. You are **FAR MORE** than simply a physical being and you are far more than simply a spirit. This time in which you live presents openings, **INCREDIBLE OPPORTUNITIES,** for you to **re-remember,** to unite with your **FULL AND AUTHENTIC SELF**.

— ARCHANGEL METATRON

SPIRITUAL BELIEFS:
HOW I BELIEVE THE UNIVERSE WORKS

Archeological records confirm that humans throughout history have sought contact with the Divine Spirit. Commonly they visualized and named various "Gods" having dominion over specific areas of their lives. As I write this text, I have an image of Lakshmi, the Hindu goddess of Abundance and Prosperity inspiring me. I don't know if this is true . . .. I just like having this image covering the rocking chair where my mother rocked me as a baby.

Religious leaders tout various ways of being and inspire their followers with these three "Laws:"

> The Law of Unity
> The Law of Cause and Effect
> The Law of Circulation

Spiritual qualities are the invisible attributes of the Divine Spirit. They are unconditional. They don't begin and end with the changeable nature of human life. I do my best to cultivate the spiritual qualities of peace, freedom, power, love, happiness, and abundance.

The Law of Unity states that we humans are all created in the likeness of the Divine Spirit. It's up to each of us to discover how to best express those qualities. Sometimes, not often, I ask the Divine for wisdom. It's hard for me to ask. I've always been smart, and that's my ego talking.

The Law of Cause and Effect states that your actions create the results you experience. The Law of Cause and Effect impacts your life in three time frames: the past, the present, and the future. By analogy, appreciate this spiritual law as expressed in ways like a mirror, a magnet, and a magnifying glass. As a mirror, what actions are reflected to you based on what you have done in the past? As a magnet, what are you attracting now via the Law of Attraction? As a magnifying glass, what future intentions did you set in Chapter III? You will be asked this question later in terms of what you intend to GIVE.

The Law of Circulation keeps energy in motion. It says, "Give your energy to change and receive a change in your experience." I was raised on a farm. My parents presented me with the old age question: "Which came first: the pheasant or the egg?" I grew up on a licensed shooting preserve. The dilemma is the same: Where do you start? Do you change your thoughts first and then the actions change? My best experience of this order came in 2016. I met a woman named Crystal who introduced herself by saying, "I help people with addictions. What's yours?" In a conversation later that day, I gave up a forty-year habit of drinking a bottle of wine a day *in one day.*

The opposite experience of changing your actions first happens regularly in Alcoholics Anonymous. AA says to put down the booze and the drugs, and your thoughts will catch up. My best experience happened within a course that centered on changing one's financial and spiritual life. During the 21-day course, we were instructed to write out a Money Purpose Statement, say it aloud with passion, and repeat this process for the entire 21 days. I wrote a short paragraph. "I create **FUN Net™ Fundraising** by devoting ≥4 hours/week creative time." This book was created out of having this thought first.

It doesn't matter which comes first if you keep the energy moving towards manifesting your intentions for your life and preserving life for all sentient beings on Mother Earth.

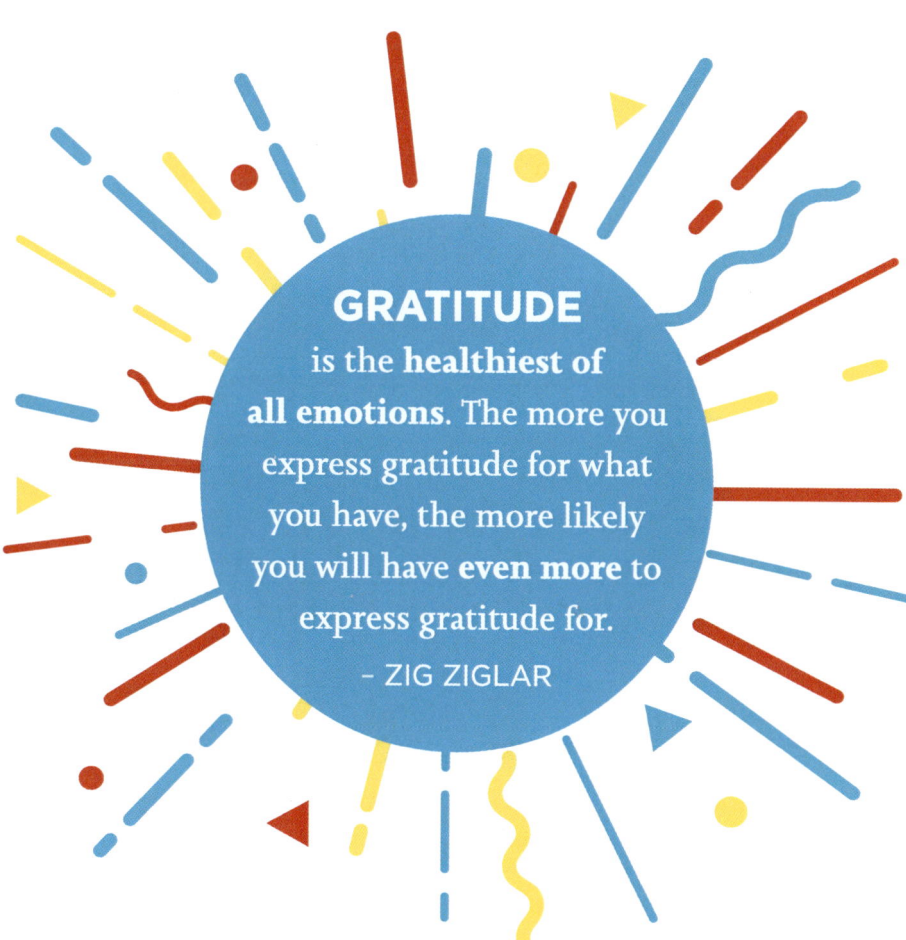

GRATITUDE is the **healthiest of all emotions**. The more you express gratitude for what you have, the more likely you will have **even more** to express gratitude for.
- ZIG ZIGLAR

MATERIAL WORLD ACTIONS:
BE • DO • HAVE • GIVE

MY RECENT BOOK, *BE DO HAVE GIVE,* shows how we can live (BE) as our material and spiritual authentic selves, take actions (DO) that show respect for others, create (HAVE) abundance, and once we have more than enough to support ourselves and our families, GIVE freely to causes we love, including preserving life sustainability on our beloved Mother Earth.

FUN Net Fundraising is a material world book set within a spiritual context. Just like you and me, this how-to book lives in the spiritual and material realms at the same time.

That's why the Archangel Metatron quote is in the Preface. You may wonder why I use the term Divine Spirit instead of the Judeo-Christian term "God." The simple explanation is that FUN people create Net Profits to support themselves and save the human race and all sentient life forms on the planet from mass extinction caused by out-of-control increasing pollution.

Quantum physicists and religious leaders agree that there is one Infinite Universe and one Divine Spirit. Everything is universally connected energy constantly in motion. We take material action in the material world to preserve our spiritual world in the context of the Universe.

BE

Bluntly, the planet needs a lot more humans willing to love and care for our human race. That is a question of **BEing** and collective consciousness

To be the change I wish to see in the world, I teach BE principles. Dave Blanchard, CEO of the Og Mandino Leadership Group, calls Kevin Hall the 21st century Og Mandino. Mr. Hall (*Aspire*) inspires these principles:

> **Genshai:** Never treat anyone small, including yourself.
>
> **Pathfinder:** Look for the signs and clues that show the best possible routes.
>
> **Namaste:** Honor everyone's God within. As it is in you, it is also within me.
>
> **Passion:** Exhibit wholehearted enthusiasm and the willingness to sacrifice for what you love most.
>
> **Sapere Vedere:** Know how to see intangibly before seeing tangibly. Believing and seeing the invisible always precedes its manifestation. ALWAYS.

Does Sapere Vedere resonate with you? If so, you know why I ask people to look for the good in everything. It's amazing what this subtle shift in perspective has on a person's level of happiness.

BE is one of the most important principles in this book. I believe this so strongly that I'm closing BE with two additional guidelines:

LIVE (BE) for the **FEELING** of **LIVING**, not to meet a schedule. Do your best to remove time from your awareness. You will **BE** present, more mindful, more often.

LIVE (BE) for the **LOVE** of **LIVING**, not for self-gain. People tend to plan in years, but they live in moments. Do your best to live in Your Moments. **Discover how much happier you are.**

HUMILITY is the bridge between BE and DO. Being humble and willing to learn facilitates growing your leadership skills.

DO

DO is about who you are **BEing** as you take action. **BE a Leader.** Five qualities (also inspired by Kevin Hall) characterize **LEADERS**.

> **Inspiring**: Breathe life into others and into their dreams as opposed to expiring or deflating others and their dreams (sucking the life out of them).
>
> **Empathy**: Walking in the path of others (walking in their shoes). Relating to all others without invoking your own boundaries or desires as to whom you relate. Showing compassion expresses empathy.
>
> **Coaching**: Literally carrying another towards her/his dreams. Think of the English Royal Family being transported in ornate coaches. Treat everyone you coach as the royalty you serve.
>
> **Ollin**: Moving forward with all your heart. In modern poker language, go **"ALL IN."**
>
> **Integrity**: Whole and complete. Leaving nothing out.

Just as we did for BE, we can rephrase these principles a bit to aid in your comprehension.

"**LIVE (DO)** to **FEEL** and **SHARE LOVE,** instead of feeling as though you need to gain something." Others will feel the love energy coming from you and will relate to you more positively.

"**LIVE (DO)** being **VITALLY INTERESTED,** not in fear." Love what you do in every moment. You will be happier, more often.

"**SPEAK (EXPRESS)** your **TRUTH** as you see it." It's your experience revealed to you for YOU to share. Only in the NOW. Spiritually, this is the only time there is.

AUTHOR'S NOTES

I'm 78 years young, in fantastic health, and need new goals. So, I created goals related to living to see the next century, related to expressing economics in 21st-century terms, and related to assuring life sustainability for all sentient beings on the planet for centuries to come.

My "not enough" childhood beliefs have faded. During the 1970s, I consulted simultaneously with over 100 medical groups. Fifteen of my clients were ex-Presidents of their medical group administrator association. My influence on two-thirds of the U.S. physicians' fees drove the Golden Age of Medicine.

My impact on the medical industry birthed my vow to transform how network marketing works . . . the business model that drives HAVE and fundraising.

HAVE as a Network Marketing Team Builder

I highly recommend network marketing as the easiest, most widely applicable business model to use in fundraising applications for lots of great reasons. The people whose actions generate income (HAVING) will BEcome customers and affiliates of a company. I train people to be efficient before/after they ever join a company. They only need to be ready to learn.

In 2019, the U.S. Office of Patents and Trademarks granted Patent #5,745,923 to Clifford Todd for Moment Time®. This is unique. It is the only patent ever granted within the network marketing industry.

As registered, Moment Time® is a six-step process:

- **FRIENDING:** Establishing or re-establishing contact with other people

- **CLARIFYING:** Exploring the friend's hopes and dreams

- **TRUSTING:** Listening to each friend's plan to achieve her or his individual goals

- **INVITING:** Asking the friend to listen to a second friend describe our company's plan

- **JOINING:** The friend says *Yes* to you; *No* or *not now* to the third person presenting the company's plan

- **PLAYER/COACHING:** Training new teammates who have agreed to join the recommended company

Implementation originally involved meeting twelve people every two weeks. I met a few three times. Mirror neuron radar-determined energetic resonance. On average, I enrolled one person every two weeks. The critical time was when the person and I established mutual trust. Even with this slower in-person process, we eliminated the long grind to achieve a six-figure income. Most new team members achieved their goals in six to nine months.

Today, in 2022, it's essential that you share solid mutual trust with everyone you invite to experience Green Fuel Global. The 2022 environment **requires** sensitivity to how you are BEing and what you are doing. **Emotions are elevated.** There's no right, no wrong, only how people filter what they see and hear through their beliefs and assign values to what they perceive, particularly since most people greet creating a six-figure residual income with skepticism.

Looking forward, I will mentor people who want to raise funds for groups of cause-driven people (e.g., congregations and non-profit environmental organizations which support efforts to preserve life for all living beings for centuries).

The ideal network marketing company for fundraising is Green Fuel Global. Why I believe Green Fuel Global is ideal is detailed in Chapters VI and VIII. In simple terms, all a person does is enroll five customers and five affiliates; then the person teaches *them* to teach their affiliates they enroll; then rinse and repeat with new affiliates who enroll to do the same things. Tools do the work. People just handle the relationships.

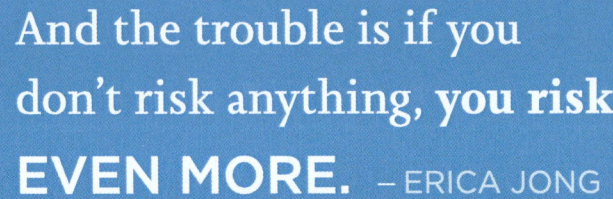

And the trouble is if you don't risk anything, **you risk EVEN MORE.** — ERICA JONG

AUTHOR'S NOTES

Legal opinions were penned by Judge Learned Hand.

"Anyone may so arrange his affairs that his taxes shall be as low as possible; he is not bound to choose that pattern which will best pay the U.S. Treasury."
— *Gregory v. Helvering*, 69 F.2d 809, 810 (2d Cir. 1934)

"Repeatedly courts have said that there is nothing sinister in so arranging one's affairs as to keep taxes as low as possible. Everybody does so, rich or poor; and all do right, for nobody owes any public duty to pay more than the law demands."
— *Commissioner v. Newman*, 159 F.2d 848, 851 (2d Cir. 1947) – dissenting opinion

HAVE as a Tax-Advantaged Taxpayer

Begin by visualizing everything you want in life—you and the Divine Spirit through you as you create all you want in life. **Sapere Vedere** said "See the intangible before it manifests tangibly. Believe in your most powerful creative force . . . your subconsciousness mind." Neuroscientists estimate that you subconsciously process 400,000 bits of information per second, while you only process 2,000 bits of information per second consciously.

You are not 200,000 times smarter than you think you are. Your subconscious computer mind has 200,000 times the computing capacity that you have consciously. Fortunately, technology makes using this computing power easy for conscious minds to use.

What's essential is the distinction: working *hard* versus working *smart* versus working *right*. A friend tells a story of a large man, proud of his strength, who felt trapped in a room. He squeezed himself into a small open window but could not make it through. He looked around and found a sledgehammer. *Ah*, he thought, *I'm smart.* He began making the opening larger. Later, he looked down a hallway, saw an open door, and walked out. At last, he discovered the right action.

It's a silly story. Except he did not sees the door until he looked around. Unfortunately, people accept what they have without looking around. Case in point: being a home-based business builder even if you go to work outside your home. It's the same with network marketing. Over the years, it abused millions of people who today refuse to look at how network marketing can be slam dunk easy. Please look around. The more you learn, the less you owe. See the **"Pathfinder"** clues and go **"Ollin."** *You'll be happy you did.*

To qualify for tax deductions, open a home-based business with the intent to make a profit. Say, "I'm opening my home-based business." Keeping track of expenses converted into tax deductions will create joy in your life.

Anyone can have a home-based business. Do you file as a single or married taxable entity? Look at a paycheck. If you're an employee, a "hunk" of it was withheld for taxes. Some of this money can launch a home-based business.

People play roles. A woman can be a daughter, wife, mother, and employee. She can also be a home-based business owner. Tax experts say that *home-based business owners are the most tax-advantaged taxpayers in America.* It's your choice: you can be multiple taxable entities at the same time.

You can be two taxable entities simultaneously. That's knowledge; e.g., looking at a GPS is knowledge. You must ACT. Choose to be BOTH.

The *2018 Tax Cuts and Jobs Act* was the first major revision of the tax code in 32 years. It invoked 53 major changes. Virtually every person and corporation in America is impacted by this legislation.

Implementing five changes provides maximum benefit for most people. My tax mentor, Dr. Ron Mueller, MBA, Ph.D., recommends that you file Form SS-4 with the IRS and get a business tax number. It's free. Tax authorities cite his work in tax court opinions. His thinking finds its way into tax law. His reference books on these strategies have been reviewed and approved by the IRS.

This chapter is based on year-end 2021 tax laws.

Your tax savings will be based on five strategies A sixth tax advantage is **zero tax liability** on 20% of your net home-based business income, but only if you satisfy conditions that are beyond the scope of this little book.

BE an instant winner: Employees can increase their tax withholding allowances, lower the tax withheld, and receive prorated portions of the lowered withholdings from that day forward until they are no longer employed. They bypass a major objection to starting your own home-based business: no available start-up capital.

Non-employees wait until their tax advantages exceed business expenses. Then they too have no negative cash flow.

Does your favorite fruit grow on trees? It takes years for a fruit tree to sprout, grow, mature and bear fruit. In contrast, a home-based business can produce positive cash flow with your next paycheck. It's your choice. Will increased positive cash flow from each paycheck inspire you? By the way, it costs your employer zero, nada, nothing.

These five tax advantages are available to all home-based business owners. I hope to inspire you to act in your own best interest. **SET CLEAR INTENTIONS.** You will achieve them . . . ONE action at a time.

1 A visibly discrete part of where you live

It can be as simple as a card table in the corner of your bedroom. To make your calculation, measure the square footage of your home office space and divide it by the total square footage of your living space. If you own your home, you can impute your business use space percentage to the total costs of owning and maintaining your home. My home office is 7' x 12' within a 400-square-foot apartment. So, 21% percent of $900 monthly rent (including utilities) is tax-deductible. Regular office equipment like computers, printers, and cell phones are tax-deductible. My purpose is to inspire you. Dr. Mueller's resource materials will educate you.

2 Your car

A key to tax savings goes into your ignition. Commuting is not deductible, but business travel from one business site to another is. The solution: confirm meeting someone for business before you leave home. An email works. Document the business conversation, date, business purpose, destination, and miles driven. Suppose you drove 20 miles. Times $.575 cents per mile creates an $11.50 deduction or $3.83 in savings for the home-based business owner. Send a thank-you email. If you need to run errands, make the reason business-related, (e.g., you need ink) and incidentally stop for groceries or what is needed. All mileage is deductible.

Keep a small notebook in your car, or text a teenager who does record-keeping. Driving 12,000 business miles per year translates into $6,900 in deductions or approximately $2,300 in real savings per year. Want a new luxury car? Claiming deductible depreciation will lower a $40,000 vehicle's real cost by 33%. That's $13,200 in taxes you don't pay. Want a big SUV or a Hummer? It gets even better.

3. Your kids, aged 7 to 17, living at home

Child labor laws protect children. Tax authorities do not see parents as likely child abusers, so you are exempt. Bottom line: employ a child and pay her or him up to $12,500 a year. Claim wages as a business expense. Banks will not open accounts for children under 18, so open custodial accounts which you control. File a tax return for each child, but since the standard deduction is $12,500, the child pays zero taxes. You pay no employee-related taxes. This is not a "gimme." You must set up a job description for each child. The child must timely record hours worked. A wall calendar works as time sheets.

What works best is **computer-savvy children** who handle record keeping, social media, media research, and the like . . . $18 to $22 per hour is the trend, but since virtual assistants command $40 to $60 per hour, the wage you pay is your choice. Document how you determined the wage rate.

Earning and saving money to buy a car is a privilege most teenagers love. Shifting up to $12,500 per year per child into non-taxable family income teaches financial awareness and saves about $4,000 in taxes payable per year.

4. Meals and travel

Business meals are 50% deductible. Keep timely records of the date, place, amount, the person(s) you are with, and the nature of the business discussion.

Combining personal and business travel follows the car logic. Never take a vacation. If the primary purpose is business, you can add in time (within limits) for pleasure.

Suppose your kids want to go to Disney World. Solution: Find a suitable convention in Orlando. Book a suite in the host hotel. Kids sleep on the pull-out bed. Lodging is tax-deductible. Buy Disney World tickets with their custodial accounts. If you want to spend a day and go to SeaWorld®, the lodging is deductible (just like stopping for groceries when the business driving purpose is to go to Staples).

Are kids' plane tickets tax-deductible? Declare the kids' plane tickets as travel to a business planning retreat and deduct them too. If you want to write off their plane tickets, put this trip in a written business plan and include child business education in the written plan.

Every $3 of personal expense you document and deduct as business expense translates into about $1 in taxes saved.

So where do you want to go? Rome? Paris? I caught the business travel bug. You'll catch it too.

5. Family health wellness care

Structure a non-taxable employee fringe benefit plan, known as a *Health Reimbursement Arrangement*. Have it professionally managed. Home-based, *single-employee businesses* can reimburse and deduct every conceivable out-of-pocket health care expense for every member of the employee's immediate family. That's right. Every conceivable health care expense for every member of the employee's immediate family. This includes health insurance premiums, co-pays, deductibles, vision expenses, dental expenses, weekly massages, nutritional supplements, acupuncture . . . the list goes on and on. Limits . . . your imagination, just document the reimbursement according to the guidelines of your plan. Zero employees? Hire yourself or your spouse, or create a C-Corp or LLC taxed as a corporation and hire yourself. A 20-year benefits management company services 10,000+ plans. Its clients' average annual income tax savings of $3,700 for individuals and $8,700 for families. The recent fee ($399) covers creating legal documents, administration for a year, and audit assistance if your plan is audited.

> **Give yourself** to something **GREATER** than you. — ROBERT S. HARTMAN LLD, PH.D.

GIVE

Giving evolves based on your ability to give and the contents of your gifts. The greatest gift you can give is your love and understanding to another by validating their human worth. Just be authentically you while you are with other people. In simple terms, **BE the real you.**

What's the best order to give? Give to yourself first by being present with yourself in the NOW. **Just BE. Enjoy Being. It doesn't get any better than this.**

Then choose how you are going to take care of your living needs. Include family's needs if you support one. Today I live alone in a small apartment in Lexington, KY.

If I can help you implement network marketing, see Resources for how to reach out to me. I'm happy to help others start their BE DO HAVE GIVE journeys to grow their abilities to support themselves, their families, their causes, and assuring life sustainability for all sentient beings on Mother Earth for centuries to come.

Let go of any technological hesitancy you may have. I am a recovering technophobe. We all can learn. One of my favorite lines from my Og Mandino coaching days was "Where dry desert ends, green grass grows."

You will always have others involved in what you do. Others (like me) can guide and teach but we are not in charge of what you choose to do. You are. You choose what you will do.

Once your income exceeds "enough," choose a heart-based project that is dear to you and begin to support it with a portion of your income stream. Continue supporting it for as long as supporting feels right to you.

I support broadcasting jazz by donating to Jazz24.org.

I support the planet's lungs breathing more freely by supporting Indigenous tribes in the Amazon Basin in their fights to shut down Big Oil's destroying the rainforest, The Pachamama Alliance is my primary funds conduit to support this cause.

I have set my intention to BE a wealthy fully-engaged activist protecting the life sustainability of our beloved planet during 2022. Please join me in these vital efforts.

We began this chapter by asking you to envision what you want. I envision moving from Lexington to a remote mountainous region where eagles procreate. I want to feel the wind beneath my imagined wings. The image of a unicorn with its wings spread inspires me. No wonder . . . I grew up on a rural horse farm in Ohio.

There were four kids in my 1st-grade class. I'm amazed when what happened decades ago is important today.

Case in point. Years ago, a U.S. Director of the Jewish Community Centers hired me to find a legal way the Centers across the country could use his nutritional drink his network marketing company produces as a fundraiser. The easiest solution is everyone donates as an individual or family out of the income earned by participating in his network marketing company. If an individual Center signed up as a distributor in his company and earned income, the IRS could count that income as "unrelated business income," which if it grew large enough, would threaten the non-profit charter of Jewish Community Centers worldwide.

Someone bought the rights to his product, so we let the effort go.

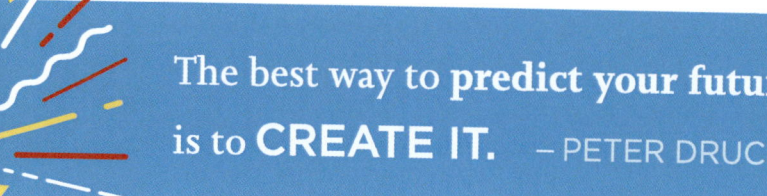

The best way to **predict your future** is to **CREATE IT.**   – PETER DRUCKER

FunNet Fundraising

AN UNFORGETTABLE, INFALLIBLE, & UNSTOPPABLE FUNDRAISER:
GREEN FUEL GLOBAL

An unforgettable, infallible, and unstoppable fundraiser easily attracts almost everyone as its supporter. Ask yourself: do you own a vehicle? Do you care about the air quality when you breathe? If you answer to both, you are ready to learn more.

People-Centered and Product-Driven *is* an unforgettable, infallible and unstoppable fundraiser. People-centered plans inspire people to take all actions that support their causes.

Product-driven means using the product rewards the "People" with funds that exceed the cost of buying the product. In essence, the **people pay themselves** each time they buy the product. Ask yourself, would you remember the cause or stop buying products **when you implicitly pay you?**

When I heard about Green Fuel Global, I thought, "Wow, these tabs would drive a perfect fundraiser for churches." I donate to non-profit organizations, so adding all non-profits was easy. I think BIG, so employee benefit plans came up next. Expressing BE DO HAVE GIVE content in this book sealed my intent. I say, "Thank you, Divine Spirit, for instilling the Green Fuel tab fundraiser into our collective consciousness."

Clifford Todd | 25

People take these actions and receive these rewards:

ACTION	REWARD
Become a customer	Access to product
Customers refer customers	Receive free product
Be a preferred customer	Receive a 10% discount
Set up monthly orders	Less time to receive products
Become a company affiliate	Access to generating funding
Affiliates engage customers	Earn %'s of their purchases
Engage new affiliates	Earn %'s of their team sales

*I've learned that people will forget what you **said**, people will forget what you **did**, but people will **NEVER FORGET** how you **MADE THEM FEEL.***
— MAYA ANGELOU

What are Green Fuel tabs and how do they work?

Green Fuel tabs are a **fossil fuel catalyst** that significantly reduces the size of fossil fuel molecules, thus vastly increasing the surface area of molecules that fire combustion engines. By analogy, think of a campfire. You use kindling to get the campfire started. That's a lot easier than trying to use just logs. The fire starts burning at a much lower temperature than an intense bonfire that burns large logs more easily.

Stay with the analogy. The morning after the campfire, you wouldn't see ashes from burned kindling, but you would see hunks of partially burned logs. In essence, more energy is released from the fuel as smaller molecules burn completely.

Using Green Fuel tabs as a fossil fuel catalyst pays its users more in savings than the users pay to buy the tabs. Tab users realize their savings via:

1. Increased mileage per gallon of fuel
2. Switching from premium to regular gasoline
3. Reduced harmful emissions
4. Diesel engines use little diesel emission fluid
5. Boosted power and performance
6. Decreased maintenance costs
7. Longer engine life (cleans out carbon deposits)
8. Improved fuel stability

Tabs come in various sizes that each treat from 10 gallons, 20 gallons, or 50 gallons. Huge commercial users can purchase Green Fuel in liquid form up to 55-gallon drums. Just drop a tab in your gas tank when you go to a gas station. It's that easy.

The Green Fuel technology is unique and required a thorough review by the Environmental Protection Agency prior to its registering Green Fuel and awarding its Seal of Approval. All ingredients in Green Fuel are sourced within the United States. Green Fuel is backed by a million-dollar liability policy. No one has filed a claim. Sounds infallible to me.

> A good plan **executed quickly** is **FAR BETTER** than the best plan executed too late. - GENERAL GEORGE S. PATTON

Observations by a Professional Fundraiser

In 1997, I joined the Orange County (CA) Chapter of the National Association of Fundraising Professionals and trained as a professional fundraiser. After 9/11, I moved to Oregon and wrote grant applications for a local community garden. Seventy-five percent of applications were funded.

I sense people dynamics as a pro fundraiser. Green Fuel users talk about their experiences by citing hard empirical data, not anecdotal evidence (e.g., "I felt better."). Supporters don't have to ask for support for their fundraiser. They go straight to conversations about common experiences. Imagine gas stations. Would you tell others about increasing miles/gallon and paying yourself by buying fuel?

People can only be registered as customers of Green Fuel Global by a customer or an affiliate. Customers able to enroll customers bypass bias against network marketing. Green Fuel Global is a new company, I'm Affiliate #38 worldwide. Its products have been used for twenty years. If the person registering a customer supports your fundraiser, the new and future sales volumes of this person are locked into your fundraiser. Since you and peer supporters need tabs for as long as you all drive vehicles, and you all keep on talking with others, new sales volumes happen. That's unstoppable.

In large companies, 25% of employees are actively looking for a new job. Most would start their own businesses if they felt they would be successful. Those who prefer to own a business can test this out as an affiliate while employed. If they leave your company to build their own business, their resulting sales volume would also be credited to your employee benefits program. In this scenario, everyone wins.

What a blessing.

> The businesses that **THRIVE** will be the ones that not only **adapt** to but also **ANTICIPATE THE POWERFUL FORCES** that are reshaping the **American marketplace.** – C. BRITT BEEMER

Our deepest fear is not that we are inadequate. Our deepest fear is that we are **POWERFUL BEYOND MEASURE.** It is our **light**, not our darkness, that frightens us most. Who am you to be **brilliant, gorgeous, talented, fabulous?** Actually, who are you not to be? You are a **Child of God.** Your playing small does not serve the world.

– MARIANNE WILLIAMSON

VII

WHAT CLIFFORD'S GUIDES TAUGHT HIM

WE RECEIVE GUIDANCE only when we are ready to receive it. Normally, our Guides speak in words we can understand, e.g., Marianne Williamson likens the energy building on the planet to the energy beneath a volcano. She says we must choose and choose soon between a violent fear-based explosion based on current societal stresses or express enough collective love for all living species and the planet that our collective futures happen non-violently. FUN Net Fundraising contributes to living non-violently.

Marianne & Clifford, 2016

My grandfather, Lester Herrick, Harvard 1896, taught me at age four to play chess. His guidance was to plan farther ahead than those who oppose you. His wisdom still guides me.

Sabine Messner introduced me to spiritual guides from my formal lives. Eric the Red was a Viking. His grandson and I would sail west until half of our food was gone. Eric told us to keep going; we would find land before we starved. Today, I always keep going. I know I'll always have enough resources. Eric the Red's grandson was Leif Ericson.

Sabine brought an English knight to my consciousness. He taught me not to draw my sword, but to keep my shield up. I follow his non-violent guidance. Sitting Bull, a Lakota Indian chief taught me to relax my reins and give my horse his head. "Trust," he said. "Your horse knows his footing better than you do." Today I trust Adrian Vashon, owner and wise CEO (LOL) and "horse owner" of Green Fuel Global.

AUTHOR'S NOTES

If you are eager to get started and are willing to take a shortcut, go immediately to #4 on page 33. Items #1 through #3 relate to how people act or feel as spiritual beings having a human experience. I've participated in New Thought-oriented churches for the last thirty years, so I guess I just assume the spiritual orientation of my friends.

Steven Covey Jr. wrote a landmark book entitled *The Speed of Trust.* He asserts that business progresses forward at a speed that is most impacted by how much the participants trust each other. That's why how much you trust someone should be your first consideration in enrolling your Green Fuel Global first-level affiliates.

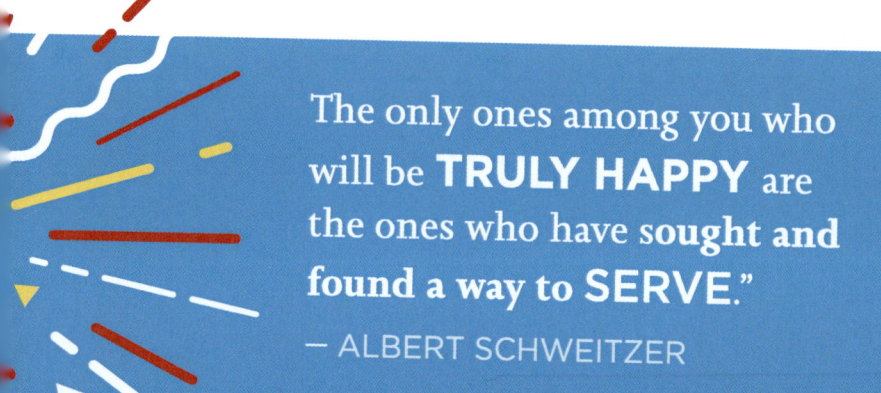

> The only ones among you who will be **TRULY HAPPY** are the ones who have **sought and found a way to SERVE**."
>
> — ALBERT SCHWEITZER

TEACHING AFFILIATES FUN NET FUNDRAISING

THE HEART OF NETWORK MARKETING IS PEOPLE. Network marketing has been, is, and always be a people relationship-based business. So, I and my FUN Net staff coach affiliates KISS: **K**eep **I**t **S**imply **S**mart.

Network marketers do two things: (1) use the products and enroll others to use the products; (2) teach those people they enroll to teach the ones *they* enroll to do the same. Said even more simply, use Green Fuel products and duplicate your efforts. That's as simple as it gets.

What are the attributes of an Ideal Affiliate?

My team and I teach our teams to enroll new people as affiliates who express the following characteristics:

1. They care about themselves. They appreciate that they are children of the Divine Spirit and, as such, unconditionally love and accept themselves just the way they are and just the way they are not. Their bodies are the way they are, and the way they are is enough and acceptable to the Divine Spirit.

2. They care about others and accept them unconditionally. They are willing to make life better for everyone.

3. They accept the necessity and power of structure including —but not limited to—the legal laws of the land.

4. You trust them, and they trust you. Others trust them. They have a circle of influence.

5. They know that 4 in 10 Americans breathe harmful polluted air. They are committed to applying their highest professionalism and best efforts to reversing the manifestation of this threat.

6. They have and keep an open mind to learning about new applications for using the Green Fuel Global opportunity. For example, they are eager to learn how to use what's presented to fund employee benefit plans abundantly and to fund private family foundations to support family-designed causes.

7. They understand and appreciate why we teach to "enroll five customers and five affiliates, and teach the affiliates to teach duplication of efforts and results five levels deep."

8. They are willing to use the tools that you/we recommend.

9. They have or can borrow as little as $225 to start up their business; $500 is the recommended start-up capital.

So, how do you find out if a person possesses these attributes? We recommend that you first introduce a sample Green Fuel tab to a prospective team member. Once she or he has experienced our fundraiser product, arrange a private conversation where you can evaluate in-depth whether you seriously want to commit yourself to having this person actively in your life for months and maybe even years.

Slow is fast. Less is more. The right five people whom, in Agape terms, you love and enroll as your first-level affiliates will, with seemingly little effort, create your abundance in monthly terms that most people only dream about in annual terms. So, take your time. Make the five best choices you can to support your life. You'll be glad you did.

Let the Tools Do the Work

Green Fuel Global provides the essential tools for you to run a lucrative business. Previously we explored Green Fuel products. Now let's explore the IDecide presentation tool and compensation plan.

The "I" is a person you want to introduce to Green Fuel Global. This tool personalizes its online presentation to the first name of your suspected future enrollee. You can send an invitation to anyone you want to either by email or text. They can watch the online presentation at their convenience and let you know what they want to do or need next. Simply, you never have to present the Green Fuel Global business opportunity. The tool does it for you. The tool sorts your "suspects" and tells you who wants to be treated as a true "prospect" for you to enroll as either a customer of or as an affiliate in your Green Fuel Global business. The tool even directs those people ready to enroll to the appropriate site where they can complete their enrollment on their own.

This tool now cuts an average person's learning time from hours per several weeks down to a couple of hours at most.

The following table is part of what an affiliate would earn when she or he completes the "five who enroll five customers and five affiliates five levels deep." Everyone buys $45 per month as Preferred Customers. It is **not a guarantee** of what you will earn once you enroll as an affiliate. It is a demonstration of the **partial** power of this compensation plan. Bonuses begin once you achieve level 3.

I've been a network marketer for fifty years. The highest single check I've ever received from a single company was $62,234. This plan is unique and more powerful than any plan I've ever seen in fifty years.

Level #	Affiliates @ $45	# Customers @ $45 Earned Dynamic Compression	% Unilevel	Monthly Compensation
You	you (1)	5	10%	$22.50
1	5	25	10%	$135.00
2	25	125	5%	$337.50
3	125	625	5%	$1,687.50
4	625	3,125	5%	$7,656.25
5	3,125	15,625	10%	$84,375.00
				$94,213,75.00

x 12 = $1,130,565 + **Bonuses**

(This could go as high as $2,000,000/year)

Please remember this is a demonstration. It is not a guarantee. What you earn is based solely on your and your team's efforts.

Is earning this range of income worth investing your time and effort to determine who your best five affiliates are and then enroll them?

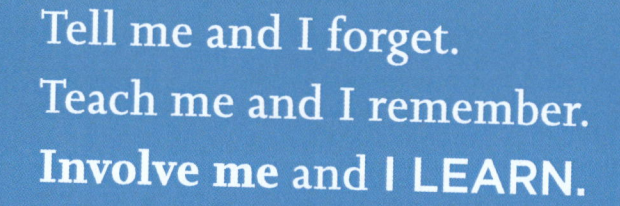

Tell me and I forget.
Teach me and I remember.
Involve me and I LEARN.
– BENJAMIN FRANKLIN

MY JOURNEY

I WANT TO SHARE a bit about my journey. I started the first grade as a farm boy in a two-room schoolhouse. I was the smallest kid in my class until college. As a senior, I repeated art appreciation and philosophy and religion classes. I'm expressing these values now sixty years later.

I enjoy "roots." My brother owns in the home where my mom (Vassar 1932) rocked me as a newborn. She and her father inspired my studying the laws of the Universe.

Setting intentions creates pivotal points in our lives. In 1966, I was in law school, but wanted to go to graduate school in economics. I set that intention. Two weeks later Rice University gave me a three-year graduate fellowship.

I lived for forty years as an alcoholic. In 2016, I met a lady who induced me to set the intention to be alcohol-free. I did so *in one day*.

Later in 2016, I vowed to re-invent network marketing. Cancer sidelined this vow. As an expert in lifestyle medicine, I self-medicated until cancer appeared to spread. I started an immunotherapy clinical trial on December 20, 2018. Fifty-six days later a biopsy could not detect live cancer cells in an enlarged cervical node. In May 2019, a PET scan could not find any evidence of cancer anywhere in my body.

Cancer freedom re-ignited my vow to enhance network marketing. In 2022, I expanded my purpose to averting mass extinction of sentient life on Mother Earth. In April 2022, I heard about Green Fuel Global. This business can yield a six-figure *monthly income stream* with less effort than most people dream annually possible. Today we are making our futures peaceful happier, loving, and abundant.

Clifford Todd

The **quality** of a person's life is **directly proportional** to their **DEDICATION TO EXCELLENCE,** regardless of their chosen field of endeavor.

– VINCE LOMBARDI

RESOURCES

Clifford Todd

Award-Winning Author, Micro-Economist
and Network Marketing Registered ® Patent Holder

clifford@cliffordtodd.com

(859) 202-1368 and **(513) 348-7872**

To talk with Clifford about Green Fuel and Fundraising:
Please text him at **859-202-1368** and request a callback.
He enjoys people and wants to know how he can best serve you.
He will call you just as soon as he is able.

715 Central Ave #C
Lexington, KY 40502

linkedin.com/in/momenttime/

facebook.com/CRexTodd

Ronald R. Mueller, MBA, Ph.D.

Home-based business tax expert and author of *Windfall Tax Savings Approved for Small Business-Owners. Home Business Tax Savings Made Easy!*
21st Edition; published 2022

Approved means reviewed and approved by the IRS.

This newest edition includes bonus chapters:
Tax Changes for 2021
Possible Changes in 2022
Taxation of Cryptocurrency 2021

To order books: HomeBusinessTaxSavings.com

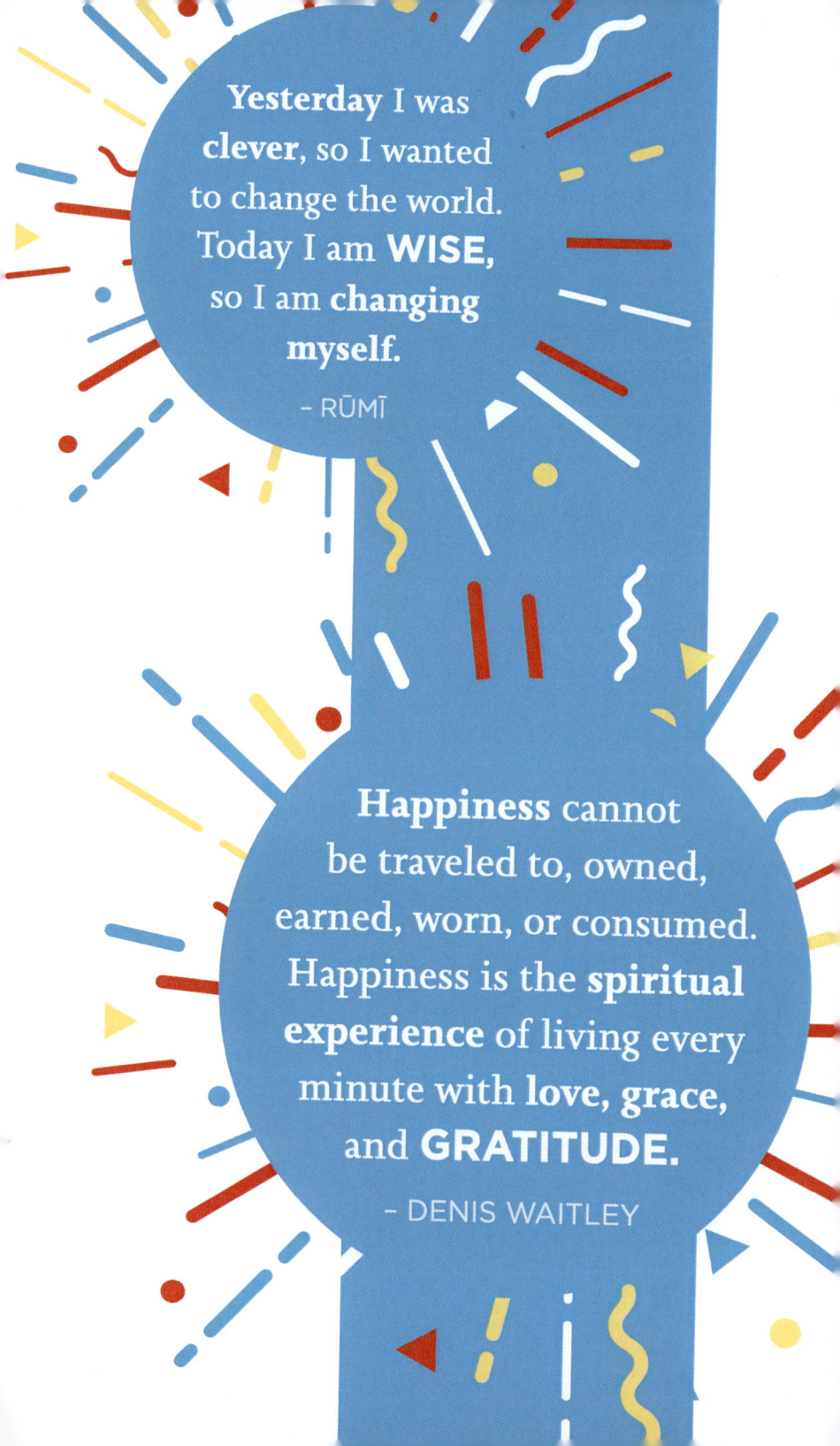

> **Yesterday** I was **clever**, so I wanted to change the world. Today I am **WISE**, so I am **changing myself.**
>
> — RŪMĪ

> **Happiness** cannot be traveled to, owned, earned, worn, or consumed. Happiness is the **spiritual experience** of living every minute with **love, grace,** and **GRATITUDE.**
>
> — DENIS WAITLEY

Made in the USA
Columbia, SC
29 July 2022